"You've never had it so good!"

A photographic record of Dagenham in the 1950s

By Susan Curtis and Gillian Gillespie

with an introduction by Tony Clifford

The London Borough of
Barking & Dagenham

Department of Education, Arts and Libraries
2001

"You've never had it so good!"

The British Prime Minister, Harold Macmillan coined the phrase "You've never had it so good!", during his premiership in the late 1950s. It reflected the country's huge economic recovery following the gloom of World War II.

This mood is mirrored clearly in the superb collection of photographs taken by Egbert Smart. On a recent trip to the Council's Archive Store, I was amazed to find over 16,000 images reflecting a quarter of a century of change from 1950 to 1975. The general public has never had such a good opportunity until now to view these pictures.

The authors have selected themes illustrating events and developments in the 1950s, such as the Coronation and the Welfare State. The text informs the reader of the national scene and the local situation in Dagenham.

This publication has the potential to interest both the general reader and local children who are studying "Britain since 1930" as part of the History National Curriculum. It also forms part of the Council's Strategy to develop and promote our rich local heritage, in which we take great pride.

Cllr. C. Fairbrass
Leader of Barking & Dagenham Council

Contents

A Photographic Record of Dagenham in the 1950s by Egbert Smart (1907-1999)

"You've never had it so good!" contains a selection of photographs taken by Egbert Smart in the 1950s. Born on 19th April 1907, Egbert won a scholarship to St Olave's Grammar School, London in 1918. There, in his own words, he "took part in compulsory athletics and cricket, and wondered what was the significance of the latter in the light of eternity"[1].

Egbert E. Smart, October 1940

He failed to matriculate, "being hopeless at maths", but his headmaster thought librarianship would make a suitable career for him[2]. Thus from 1925 to 1928 he attended University College School of Librarianship, London, where he received the Sir John McAllister Medal for Best Student. From 1928 to 1931 he worked at the Medical Society Library. Within the first hour of working there, Egbert recalled how a surgeon came in and apologised for the delay in returning a book, which his father had borrowed in 1878! He also described how "one evening, groping for a light switch, I knocked a man's severed arm off a dish onto the carpet. On another occasion, I found on my table a woman's heart with a safety pin sticking into it. Apparently the woman had been changing her baby's nappy, had held the pin in her lips for a moment and accidentally swallowed it. The sharp point had penetrated the wall of the oesophagus and pierced her heart".

In 1930, Egbert wrote a play entitled "Gobbo Hys Boke Seleccyon" which was performed in the Botanical Theatre with great success. Following a recommendation from Dr Baker, Director of the School of Librarianship, he joined the editorial team of Routledge's *Guide to the Best Fiction in English*. Egbert considered it to be "hack work and a waste of my eye-sight". He pulled out of this project, but began work on their *Guide to the Best Historical Fiction in English*.

Egbert was asked by a friend in 1941 to work on a temporary basis for Dagenham Public Libraries due to a staffing crisis occasioned by the War. Thus began his long association with this area. During the winter of that year Egbert cycled through the snow to attend his army medical in Colchester. He was graded 5a and his call-up was deferred. His father told him later that the attending physician, a longstanding friend of his, had written to say that he was "basically a philosopher".

He became a Fellow of the Library Association in 1944[3] and was put in charge of Wantz Library, a new branch, where every Monday he chaired a lively discussion group. Here he met Marion, "recently demobbed", and they married on 5th April 1950. He moved to work at Rectory Library in 1960, where he remained until his retirement in 1972. Dagenham Branch Libraries were regarded as cultural centres and Egbert was the local contact for Rectory Music Circle and Fanshawe Film Society[4].

His father had always been interested in photography and "gave Egbert a camera hoping he would be interested too. He didn't expect to be but he took the camera with him on a ski-ing holiday thinking that some of the others would like to use it. No one took much interest but Egbert managed to take one roll over the following days. He had this developed at the resort and was delighted with the results. With this encouragement he took a dozen more rolls before the end of the holiday. He was hooked!"[5].

As an enthusiastic photographer, Egbert was a founder member of the Dagenham Co-operative Film Society, which started in 1947. He was Secretary for several years and wrote the programme notes which accompanied the meetings at

Valence House. The Society made some notable films of its own including "The Seeds of Time"[6], which Egbert directed. "Our Year", filmed in 1957-58, was concerned with memorable events in Dagenham and gained a two-star award in the Amateur Cine World Annual Competition. He was also responsible for the titles of the four-star award winning colour film "Piccadilly Circus".

In August 1951 Egbert was officially appointed as the Council's Photographer[7] and he began recording the modern development of Dagenham. His role was to snap " every aspect of the Borough's life, from uneven pavements to royal visitors". He took photographs for all Council Departments, on the understanding that developing and processing was carried out by professional photographers (Vincent Ltd, Ilford), and that requests for his services were made in writing, or by telephone if urgent, to John Gerard O'Leary, the Chief Librarian. As a consequence, thousands of photographs were taken that otherwise could not have been afforded. For this extra duty, Egbert received an honorarium of £40 a year.

Egbert E. Smart, March 1957

Egbert's daughter, Susan, as Consort to the Mayor of Dagenham!

The General Purposes Committee purchased four cameras for Egbert's use: an Ensign (used mainly for colour work), a Rolleiflex[8], a Kodak Special (a plate camera, used mainly for copying documents) and a Rolex 16mm Cine Camera. This Committee paid for the cost of raw films, contact prints and albums for storage. Twenty bound volumes of these images are stored today at Valence House Museum.

Browsing through these albums, we find photographs of carnivals, sporting events, street parties, swimming galas, special occasions and ceremonies. We meet distinguished foreign and other visitors to the Borough. We observe damage to public property and sites for town planning applications and appeals. There are medical photographs of antenatal, geriatric and other treatments at local clinics[9]. Nearly all Council Departments found a use for the service – the Shops Acts Inspector when making prosecutions or the Borough Architect recording building work.

Local history fascinated Egbert and he wrote many articles in the *Dagenham Digest* signed "E.E.S.". "Job Changing in Dagenham" (no.25, 1954), "The Population of Dagenham" (no.33, 1956), "The Workers of Dagenham a Hundred Years Ago" (no.22, 1954), "Thomas,

1st Lord Denman, Lord Chief Justice of England" (no.23, 1954), and "Dagenham – Then and Now" (no.30, 1956) are good examples of his contribution. During the 1950s and 1960s, Egbert assisted John O'Leary in staging exhibitions illustrating Essex history.

Colleagues remember Egbert's dry sense of humour, which he demonstrated on one occasion by producing a double exposure showing the ghost of Agnes de Valence in the grounds of Valence House[10]. The "ghost" was, in fact, his daughter Susan. This was published in the *Dagenham Digest* [11] and resulted in several reported sightings of the ghost by local residents. Some of his photographs seem amusing today, but were taken with a serious intention. These include the man stuck up a tree who turns out to be innocently pruning on behalf of the Parks Department[12] and the sludge-hopper for a primary sedimentation tank described as an "abstract sculpture by Ben Nicolson" [13].

Many of Egbert's photographs record buildings now gone – for example, Comyn's Cottages [14] in Dagenham Village. Others have great charm and reveal a talent for capturing the perfect moment [15]. Many of his studies of children are particularly good examples of his photographic prowess [16]. Susan

Egbert and Marion with their grandaughter

Walby, Egbert's daughter, remembers how her father was meticulous in recording the life of the Borough, often taking her and her brother with him. "In our childhood, events were as enthusiastically recorded. There were times when my brother and I thought events had been planned solely for the photo opportunity they presented, such was Daddy's pleasure in photography. He always made sure his children had cameras and then wanted to see the results when the prints were made". Despite the changes in camera technology over the years, Egbert maintained his interest in the creative process, but was astonished in his later years that taking a photograph had become so easy. He was bemused to see his young grandchildren with their first cameras taking competent pictures at the age of 6, with no knowledge of light meters, tripods, flash bulbs, lenses, filters, f-stops, plates or boxes of film.

Egbert Smart died on 8th January 1999, aged 91. His photographic legacy however lives on and it is hoped that this book will recapture the spirit of Dagenham in the 1950s.

Tony Clifford

1   Personal account by Egbert Smart, 8 April 1997.
2   "Life, Love and Librarianship", a talk given by Egbert Smart to the English Speaking Union in 1996.
3   *Library Association Yearbook*, 1964.
4   *Borough of Dagenham: Directory of Local Organisations and Activities*. 1964.
5   Correspondence from Susan Walby, Egbert's daughter.
6   *Dagenham Digest*, no.45, 1959.
7   Most of what follows is taken from reports by J. G. O'Leary, Chief Librarian of Dagenham from 1928 to 1965.
8   According to his daughter, Egbert had to apply for a permit to import the Rolleiflex from West Germany. He used this camera and the two others until his retirement in 1972.
9   For example, "The School Health Service", *Dagenham Digest*, no.29, 1955.
10 The ghost picture was taken using the plate camera, the only one that did not have a mechanism to prevent double exposure.
11 "Up Spirits!" *Dagenham Digest*, no.72, 1966.
12 *Dagenham Digest*, no.27, 1955.
13 *Barking Record*, no.70. 1966.
14 *Barking Record*, no.77, 1968.
15 "Fishing in the Moat at Valence House". *Dagenham Digest*, no.41, 1958.
16 For example, "Dagenham children, worth doing something for". *Dagenham Digest*, no.57, 1962.

Village Life

England's traditional rural way of life had radically changed during the inter-war years. The construction of the massive Becontree Estate had swallowed the agricultural landscape of Dagenham. Small rural enclaves survived in the parish in the 1950s but these were urbanised by new housing estates such as Marks Gate and Heath Park during this period. Near St. Peter and St. Paul's Parish Church on the edge of the Becontree Estate some semblance of village life continued. Old buildings still remained in the heart of Dagenham Village but even these were soon to disappear during "re-development" in the 1960s.

Dagenham Vicarage, 1956

A bird's eye view of Dagenham Village from the Church Tower, 1954

The Parish Church of St. Peter and St. Paul in the heart of Dagenham Village

A typical Essex weatherboarded cottage in Dagenham, 1956

A village view, 1952

The village gather for King George VI's Memorial Service in Dagenham Parish Church, 1952

Down on the Farm

By the 1950s the major cities of England were expanding and new towns such as Basildon and Harlow were being built. This move continued the progression from a rural to urban lifestyle for many people. In Dagenham agriculture was a major industry until the 1920s when the majority of farms were compulsorily purchased by the London County Council to build the Becontree Housing Estate.

The surviving farms in Dagenham at this time were situated in the little hamlet of Marks Gate, to the north of the Eastern Avenue. By the end of the fifties, with the construction of a new housing estate, even they had disappeared. In the 21st century, only Furze survives as a working farm. However, some of the old farmhouses such as Bentry Heath, Raydons, Pettits and Warren still stand surrounded by municipal housing.

Timber beams in the barn at Bentry Heath Farm, 1953

Rose Lane Farm at Marks Gate, 1951

'Dagenham's green and pleasant land.'

Mill Farm in Whalebone Lane North, Chadwell Heath, 1953

'We plough the fields and scatter'

'Feeding the chickens'

Raydons Farmhouse, 1953

A Brighter Future

A hundred years after the Victorians' Great Exhibition the Festival of Britain opened in 1951 on the south bank of the Thames. This decade heralded a new era of optimism following the difficult war years. The national focus was a huge exhibition in London, which displayed Britain's progress in art, science, industry and architecture. This was organised to encourage the nation to look forward to a brighter future.

'All dressed up!'

'Tuck in!'

'Our Street – Downing Road'

The Dagenham Digest of September 1951 reported that "all over England, big places and little places have celebrated the feast. There has been a simple humble patriotism that we can all admire and everyone can copy". Dagenham residents enjoyed a month long festival of entertainment launched on the 3rd of June with an open-air church service. The programme included a carnival, a pageant, music festivals and numerous street parties.

Expectations were high with ordinary people anticipating the beginning of a new age of prosperity.

'Fun and games'

Alderman Mrs Evans plants a festival tree in Central Park

'Happy days are here again!'

Festival of Britain Pageant at Valence Moat

A **Sign** of the **Times**

Commercial television was launched on the 22nd of September 1955. Rather than being funded by a licence this new venture drew income from advertising. The first advert broadcast was for Gibbs SR toothpaste.

In the Dagenham area, large roadside hoardings were constructed to advertise everyday products. Many of these goods are still used regularly today, such as Ovaltine and HP Sauce.

'Sitting amongst the signs' in Rainham Road South, 1956

'Let's have a Coke!'

Hoarding at the Merry Fiddlers' Junction, 1954

Strong opinions were held regarding political issues of the day including those by members of the 'Dagenham Campaign for Nuclear Disarmament'. The slogan "Hands off Korea" appeared daubed on walls in the area to protest against this conflict. The Korean War fizzled out in the early months of 1953 much to public relief.

Local working conditions and public services were also high on the agenda.

'Improve our working conditions'

'Read all about it!'

'Anti-war protest'

'Ban the Bomb'

Baby Boom

'Ladies in Waiting', 1959

Mothers and children at Oxlow Lane Clinic, 1958

'In the weighing room!'

In the post-war era, the birth rate soared as couples "caught up" on the lost years! Infants benefited greatly from the provision of the newly established National Health Service.

New immunisation programmes could now more effectively treat diseases, which were child-killers earlier in the century. For example, the polio vaccine introduced in 1956 dramatically reduced paralysis and mortality rates. Cases of tuberculosis and diphtheria were dramatically reduced in Dagenham as the Health Service implemented a series of preventative measures. The Dagenham clinics like others in the country were active in spearheading this progress.

Poliomyelitis lecture at Wantz Library, 1956

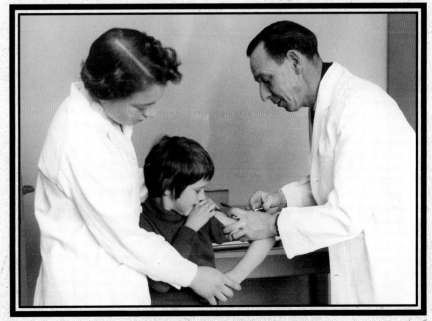

As an example to others, Dr Gillet injects his own daughter with the polio vaccine

'A precious bundle'

God save the Queen

'Putting the flags out!'

Preparing for the street party in Beverley Road

'Rule Britannia!'

On June 2nd 1953, Queen Elizabeth II was crowned in Westminster Abbey. Throughout the realm factories, offices and schools were closed. Despite the cold wet weather two million people travelled to London to see their new Queen. Meanwhile history was also in the making as many gathered to watch this event for the first time on television.

In towns like Dagenham, street parties were held and children were given Coronation mugs to remind them of the day. The Borough Council provided £5,000 for its week of Coronation celebrations, which culminated in a carnival procession and "a magnificent firework display presented by the Ford Motor Company".

The second 'Elizabethan Age' heralded a new spirit of optimism following the difficult years of the Second World War.

'Showtime' in Monmouth Road

Coronation Carnival Procession at the junction of Wood Lane and Beverley Road

'Coronation Can-Can!'

'Fireworks over Dagenham'

The Best Days of our Lives

In the early 1950s rationing of clothing and food was still in force. However, much to the delight of children in 1953 they could at last buy as many sweets as they liked! In the following year, rationing ceased on all goods.

This was a decade of great change and Britain became a prosperous society with plenty of money to spend. Dagenham Urban District Council invested in many new leisure facilities such as a new playground in St. Chad's Park which greatly benefited local children. In 1950 playing fields were reinstated after being used for food production during the war.

'Babes in the Wood!'

'The Ocean Wave'

'Jumping Beans!'

Playleadership Scheme in Old Dagenham Park, 1958

In comparison with today this was an age of innocence. It was safe for children to play in the parks and on the streets without adult supervision. In the school holidays play-leadership schemes such as in Old Dagenham Park were organised to keep youngsters amused. An article in the Dagenham Digest of September 1959 relates that the scheme aimed to "encourage the team spirit, help children who fight shy of others, encourage leadership and, above all, keep children out of mischief". Happy summer days were also spent by young people in the open-air swimming pools in Valence and Leys Parks.

As the 1950s drew to a close the influence of popular music and films featuring idols such as Elvis Presley and James Dean resulted in the "teenage revolution". Life would never be the same again!

'Queuing up!'

'Me and my Shadow'

'The Water Babies'

A Class Act

'All things bright and beautiful' Hymn Practice, 1957

The Dancing Class, 1955

'The ten times table.'

Due to the "baby boom" many more children were ready to attend full time education in the early 1950s. Many schools with modern equipment were built for them. Marks Gate Infants and Junior Schools situated at Lawn Farm Grove were officially opened in 1957 to serve the new housing estate. Every primary school pupil was given a free bottle of milk at morning break and the School Meals Service provided cooked dinners often consisting of meat, two vegetables and steamed pudding and custard.

The 1944 Education Act meant that children had to attend school until the age of fifteen. To decide which school they should go to children sat an examination called the "eleven plus". About 20 per cent passed and went to grammar schools with the expectation that they would progress to higher education. Those who failed went to secondary modern schools to equip them for manual and clerical jobs.

One of the schools attended by Dagenham youngsters was Bishop Ward in Wood Lane, opened as a co-educational secondary modern in 1954. Grammar school candidates went to Dagenham County High in Parsloes Avenue. Perhaps the most famous ex-pupil of this establishment was Dudley Moore, the entertainer, who won an organ scholarship to Magdalen College, Oxford. He graduated in 1958 with two degrees – B.A. and B. Mus.

Exhibition of pupils' work at Robert Clack Technical School, 1956

Schools' Speech Festival, 1956

'Playtime' at Dagenham County High

'We're all going on a summer holiday!'

A Spoonful of Sugar

The new National Health Service provided free treatment by doctors, dentists and opticians. As a result people gradually became fitter. In 1951 smallpox broke out but fortunately an epidemic was avoided by inoculation. As some problems were solved others appeared, for example industrial pollution caused "smog" in large cities. In 1952, four thousand people died as a result of a London smog. Dagenham householders were encouraged to use smokeless fuel and the council maintained an observation station which measured atmospheric pollution.

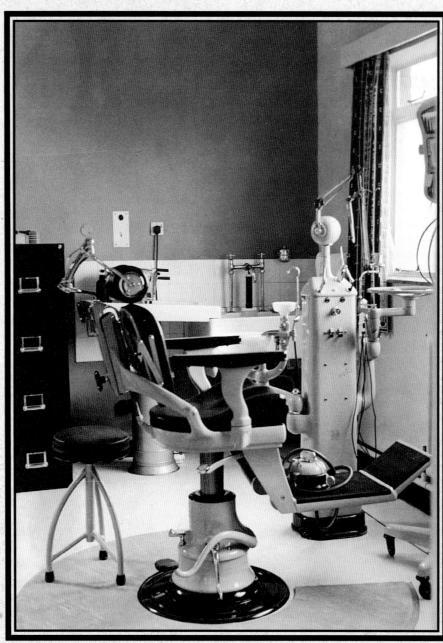

'The Dentist's Chair'

'All's clear!'

'Breathe in!'

The School Health Service in Dagenham provided comprehensive medical examinations for each pupil. The most common defects found in Dagenham children in 1955 were bad teeth, poor vision and chronic infections in ears, nose and throat. Less common in this period was malnutrition and lice infestation.

'A little ray of sunshine!'

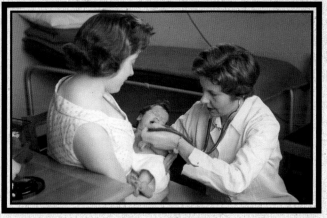

'Doing fine!'

'Repeat after me'
Speech therapist recording girl's progress, 1955

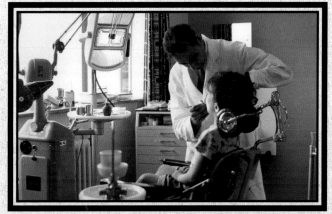

'Open wide'

Home Sweet Home

In the 1950s new materials and methods of building had been developed. Steel window frames, asbestos slates and concrete tiles were all used. To provide accommodation quickly to support urgent housing needs, pre-fabs were constructed. Thousands were put up in the early 1950s and were intended to last ten years. People took great pride in their new homes and in Dagenham some of these temporary buildings boasted competition-winning gardens.

'A modern kitchen, 1958'

'A prefab to be proud of', 1956

Trefgarne Road
on the Heath Park Estate, 1953

A good example of a new housing scheme was the Heath Park Estate which received a Festival of Britain Architectural Award – only seventeen of these were given out all over the nation. In the newly built properties, kitchens and bathrooms had a constant hot water supply. This was considered a very modern innovation. New machines and gadgets like refrigerators and washing machines had been invented prior to the war. However, it was not until the fifties when mass-production resulted in price reductions, that the average family was able to afford such luxuries.

'Dolly's Bathtime – water's hot!'

'Relaxing in the garden'

'Happy Birthday to you!'

'Goodnight sweetheart'

Tiptoe through the Tulips

During World War II, the dig for victory campaign encouraged the nation to use all available land to grow food. This movement continued into the 1950s at which time allotments were a popular means of growing fresh produce for all the family. In 1951, there were around 2,500 allotments being cultivated in Dagenham.

Many councils encouraged residents to tend their gardens, regular competitions being held to select the best. In Dagenham, civic pride was raised by encouraging people to look after gardens to improve the local environment.

The horticultural display at the annual Town Show was a major event, with exhibitors presenting "gigantic marrows, long orange carrots, pyramids of pearly onions and festoons of beans". Perhaps this was the beginning of the organic gardening movement!

'Pick of the crop'

Interior of greenhouse in Central Park, 1957

Beacontree Heath allotments, 1953

A prize winning garden, 1956

'Know your onions!', Town Show, 1959

Inside the Horticultural Tent at the Town Show, 1953

'A bountiful harvest', Town Show, 1951

The **Butcher, Baker** and the **Candlestick Maker**

At the start of the fifties, shopping involved visiting individual specialist shops on an almost daily basis. Many housewives however, still relied upon street traders to deliver goods and services directly to their homes. The mikman was a regular visitor arriving early each morning with fresh milk for all the family.

In 1950, the first self-service shop opened in Britain and by the end of the decade most large towns had a supermarket. There was government concern in 1956 that women would be "lured into over-spending" in these new self-service outlets.

'Variety is the spice of life.'

*'Off to the shops',
at Dagenham Heathway, 1953*

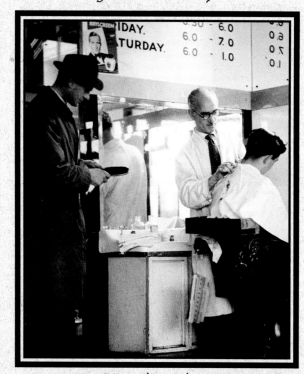

'A visit to the Barber', 1951

30

Unlike the national picture, Dagenham had been planned without a central shopping centre and relied mainly on small local parades of shops. These provided a personal service to customers, weighing and cutting food to order. Today it is interesting to discover that it was not until 1952 that Dagenham food stores were instructed by the council to request customers to leave dogs outside!

'Buy me an ice-cream, please!'

'A parade of shops' in Broad Street, 1953

'The milk round', 1951

Mr Wright – the Shop Inspector at work, 1956

A Woman's Work is Never Done!

'Mrs Average Housewife and her family'

'Kitchen Capers', at Wantz Restaurant, 1957

Food hygiene lecture for Bartons Bakery staff in Kent Road, 1957

During World War II, many women worked to help the war effort. As the men returned to civilian life their wives concentrated on the home and bringing up the family. A Mass Observation Pilot Study of 1951 reported that "Mrs Average Housewife" had a normal working day of 15 hours. This added up to a 75-hour week and overtime was still required on Saturdays and Sundays!

Only 21 per cent of the Dagenham workforce was female in 1954. The majority of these were employed in part-time unskilled jobs in factories and the catering industry. Major local employers included May and Bakers Chemical Factory and Bartons Bakery. The local authority also employed women in secretarial and clerical posts.

Printing the Council's minutes, 1957

'Working on the accounts'

Serving a young customer at Wantz Library, 1956

Danger – Men at Work!

During this decade for the first time workers did not need to fear poverty if they were ill or out of work. The National Insurance Scheme had been set up in 1948 and ensured that employees received regular payments when they retired, were sick or unemployed. Times were good for men returning to work from the services. British industry was thriving once more and there were major projects to build houses, roads and factories. Post war working conditions especially in factories were much cleaner and safer.

'Relaying the road' at Hog Hill, 1954

'Are you alright, mate?'
Redecorating Valence House, 1957

'Mind your head!'
Pruning roadside trees, 1955

Dagenham had a varied industrial base including the Ford Motor Company and Southern United Telephone Cables Ltd. Dagenham Council was also a major employer, which directly maintained the municipal housing stock on the Becontree Estate. Major road works resulted from further urbanisation programmes including a new by-pass for Dagenham Village. Many were employed in labour intensive tasks such as culverting the Wantz Stream which today would be quickly completed by heavy machinery.

'Down in the Dumps!'
Culverting Wantz Stream, 1954

'Hard labour!'
Road repairs in
Chadwell Heath, 1957

'Tea's up!'

'What a load of old rubbish!'

The **Wheels** on the **Bus**

Buses and coaches were a popular means of daily travel. Other services like the tram were gradually declining as streets became busier. Double-decker buses were driven by a man in a separate cab and a conductor who collected fares and helped passengers. One of the most popular bus routes for Dagenham residents was the one to Romford on market days. At the weekends, people could easily visit the countryside at nearby Hainault Forest by bus.

'Whoosh!', Chequers Lane, 1958

'Double Deckers'
at Beacontree Heath Bus Station

'On the top-deck'

For longer journeys people would travel by train on the recently nationalised "British Railways". In 1955, steam locomotives began to be replaced by diesel or electric ones. Dagenham was well served by underground and main line services. Locals could easily travel to London for work and to Southend for family outings.

Air travel had always been too expensive for ordinary people but in 1955 cheap tourist flights were introduced to France and Spain. A week-long inclusive break in Paris was available for as little as £24! Meanwhile the village of Benidorm on Spain's Costa del Sol was described by a travel writer in 1957 as being "charming and not yet spoilt by easy money".

'Full steam ahead'

'Waiting for the train'

'Day trippers'

'Traffic Jam'

On the Move

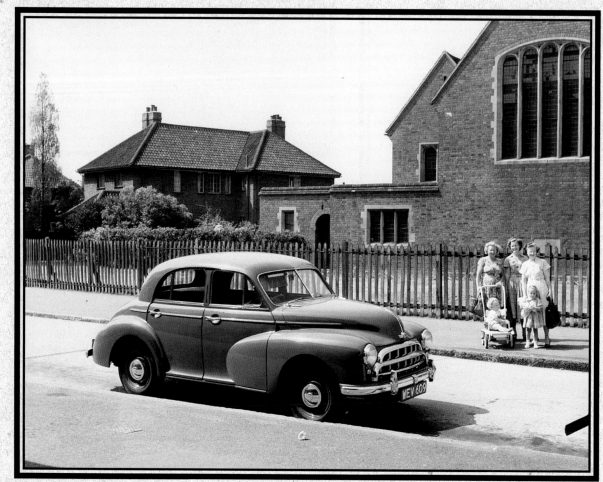

'A classic car being admired!'

'Car lot'

Scooter Rally in Central Park, 1959

For the first time in history at the close of the 1950s ordinary people could travel freely without relying on public transport. Over five million households owned a car, which put pressure on the inadequate road network. A four-year plan costing £212 million to create new motorways was launched in 1955 with the first stretch opening between London and Birmingham in 1959.

Towards the end of the decade motor manufacturers developed innovative solutions such as the 'bubble' and 'mini' cars to enable more people to afford to take to the roads. The traffic warden scheme was introduced in 1956 to relieve the police of some of their traffic duties.

People were still used to getting about on their own two feet. Many still cycled or rode scooters to work. Roads however became increasingly dangerous places and as Dagenham became more urbanised schemes such as the Road Safety Week were successfully introduced to deal with this issue.

'Far from the madding crowd...'

'The Silent Street', Winding Way, 1953

'On your bike!'
Outside May & Bakers chemical factory, 1952

Road Safety float, 1953

Match of the Day

'The Winning Team' – Ford's Football Club, 1953

'Team talk'

'Howzat!' – Old Dagenham Cricket Club

Every weekend crowds of spectators gathered at football matches and other sporting events. An achievement which caught the public imagination, in 1954, was Roger Bannister "running the mile" in under four minutes for the first time in history. In the same year at the Empire and Commonwealth Games in Vancouver, local athlete Jim Peters caused a sensation by collapsing just before the finish of the marathon race. At the time he was the greatest marathon runner in the world but sadly never competed again and returned to continue his profession as an optician in Chadwell Heath.

Other local sporting heroes growing up in the Dagenham area in the 1950s include Jimmy Greaves, Martin Peters and Terry Venables.

In the days before mass media, most people participated in sport as a leisure activity. One of the most popular in this area was angling which took place at Valence Moat.

Angling at Valence Moat, 1957

'Run for your life!'

'On the green!'

'Tee-ing off!'
The Official Opening of St Chad's Golf Course, 1955

It's That Time of Year Again

A major part of Dagenham's heritage, which started in the fifties, has been the annual Town Show and Carnival held in Central Park each summer. Its success has relied on the enthusiasm of local residents as the Dagenham Digest noted in 1956, "it is a great thing to bring together thirty-thousand friends and neighbours".

'Beauty afloat', Dagenham Parks Department entry, 1955

'Under canvas' for the 1952 Town show

'Not rain again!', Town show, 1955

The show was popular with all sections of the community. "The carnival went off with a bang and proved a very pleasant diversion on a fine Saturday afternoon" reported the Dagenham Digest referring to its success in 1954. Exhibits ranged from lace making to cage birds and from dog shows to dahlias. A wide variety of hobbies were displayed including bee keeping, aquaria and crafts. There was a trade exhibition, a fun fair and "the loveliest of all sights – a firework display".

'If you want to get ahead, get a hat!', Town show arena, 1953

'Watching the show'

Winners of the Robert Clack Trophy, 1955

'Let me out!'

All the Fun of the Fair

One of the most popular forms of entertainment for the whole family was the traditional fun fair. The equipment for these events was transported from town to town by groups of travellers. This was the decade in which great changes began to take place eventually resulting in the theme park craze so popular today. In 1955, Walt Disney opened "Never-Never Land" near Los Angeles, which we now know as "Disneyland". In time this led to the development of larger static fairs with more thrilling attractions which appealed to a much wider audience.

The annual Dagenham Town Show and any special occasion like the Coronation always had an accompanying fair. Local people flocked to Central Park to try their skills on the sideshows and ride on the big wheel.

'Helter-Skelter'

'Carousel'

'Swing Low, Sweet Chariot!'

'On the Big Wheel'

'Punchball'

'A Bird in a Gilded Cage!'

'Dagenham Illuminations'

That's Entertainment!

In today's world the choice of entertainment available is endless. This was not the case prior to World War II. Activities mainly based in the home included such pastimes as playing card games and Sing-alongs around the piano. After the war, things gradually began to change. People had more time to spend in leisure pursuits. In Dagenham the Arts Council, set up in 1949, arranged a wide range of opportunities for members of the community. Whatever your interest there was an arts event for you to participate in. You could join the choral society, the Valence Theatre Group, attend a municipal dance or listen to the "Holiday Orchestra" conducted by Dr. Swinburne.

'Swan Lake', the Donna Roma Ballet Troupe performing in the grounds of Valence House, 1953

'The Circus comes to Town...'

'In the Mood!'.
Municipal dance in Leys Hall, 1951

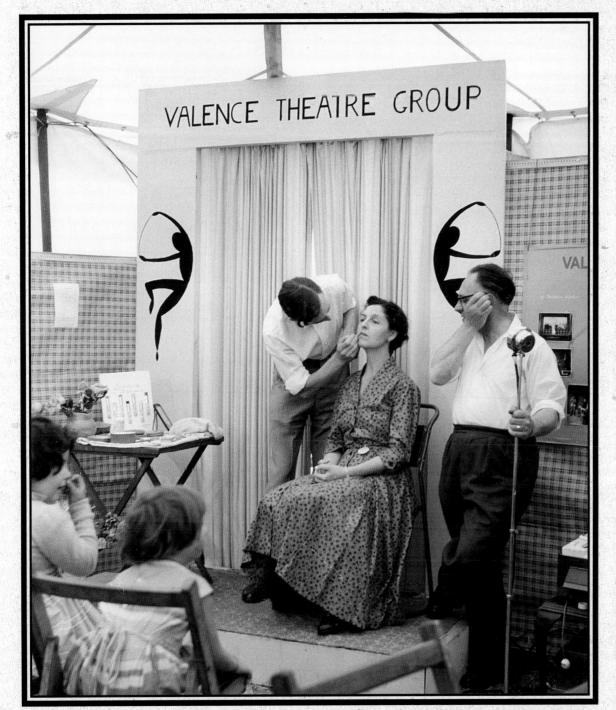

'The Make-Up Department of Valence Theatre Group'

'Hallelujah!'. Dagenham Choral Society performing Handel's Messiah at Central Hall, Heathway, 1957

'Black Chiffon', a scene from the play presented by Valence Theatre Group at Halbutt School, 1954

'A classical trio'

The Swirl of the Kilt

The 1950s were the heyday of the Dagenham Girl Pipers. They began as a small group from Dagenham Congregational Church organised by Rev. Graves in 1930. Soon they became internationally famous and performed all over the world. Just before the outbreak of war in 1939 they had a lucky escape from Nazi Germany. To boost national morale in the early 1940s they travelled far and wide to entertain the troops.

Their national popularity continued in the 1950s and they were an integral part of entertainments provided to mark major events such as the Festival of Britain and the Coronation. "Their popularity was unbounded" reported the Dagenham Digest in October 1955 as they celebrated their Silver Jubilee.

'In training!'

'A superb performance', at Valence Moat, 1951

'On parade' in Dagenham Village

'Marching in formation'

'A feather in your cap!'

'The sound of the bagpipes'

'The alternative Girl Pipers!'

Bookworms

At the beginning of the 1950s, very few families had a television in their home. Favourite pastimes included listening to the radio and reading books. Most children had a favourite comic such as the Eagle or Girl and an eagerly awaited radio adventure story such as Dick Barton – Special Agent, which usually ended on a cliff-hanger.

People could not afford to buy many books and few paperbacks were available. A pioneering library service for Dagenham was established by John Gerard O'Leary, which provided excellent opportunities to access a wide range of educational resources.

'Storytime with Daddy'

'Parental guidance!'

'Serious students'

'An avid bookworm'

Story hour with Miss Ormrod, 1955

'Meeting the Mayor', Official Opening of the
Children's Library at Dagenham Branch, 1958

The Hospital Library Service at Rush Green, 1956

Making an Exhibition of Yourself

'Dressing up!'

'Is anybody there?'

Girls from Dagenham County High School visit the Stuart Essex Exhibition, 1956

An outstanding series of themed exhibitions on Essex history were organised by Dagenham Public Libraries during the 1950s. Subjects ranging from the Saxons to the Victorians were displayed in the museum room at Valence House, which was the headquarters of the Libraries Department. Today museum visiting has become a popular leisure activity with multi-media and interactive displays to attract the modern child. In contrast these photographs show visiting school parties interacting with artefacts presented in a simple way.

It was amazing that the local community were able to see such rare and valuable collections, loaned from a wide range of organisations. Normally they would have had to visit the Tower of London to see suits of armour, the British Museum for ancient manuscripts and the National Portrait Gallery for paintings. These items and many others were seen in Dagenham due to the persuasive powers of John Gerard O'Leary, the innovative Chief Librarian.

'Alas, poor Yorick!'

'Mr O'Leary displays his wares!'

'More tea, vicar?', Official Opening of the Georgian Essex Exhibition, 1958

'A study in concentration'

Animal Affairs

'Fox and hounds'

'Nellie the Elephant!'

'In the rabbits' hutch!'

Since the 1950s public attitudes to animals and traditional rural pursuits have radically altered. In 1957 a demonstration of fox hunting was well received at the Horse Show in Central Park. Although this locality was mostly urbanised by this time the vestiges of traditional rural life and links with the Essex countryside remained strong. Such an event today would cause certain uproar and protest, as would the entertainments provided by exotic animals.

Organisations such as the People's Dispensary for Sick Animals (P.D.S.A.) provided care and attention to much treasured pets. This organisation served the Dagenham community during the fifties from a building previously used as the Robin Hood Inn in Bennett's Castle Lane.

'White Beauties!'

'You little monkey!'

'Talk to the animals!'
A llama parades in Dagenham, 1951

P.D.S.A. in Bennett's Castle Lane, 1955

It's a **Dog's Life!**

'Judging – a very serious matter!'

'My dog is better than yours!'

'Standing to attention!'

A vital element of the Town Show festivities was the annual dog show, which started in 1953. A separate class was even held for children showing their beloved pets. Judging was a very serious matter with pampered pooches often misbehaving causing great dismay for their owners. Much time and effort went into preparing each animal for its moment of glory!

'Behave yourself – you're on show!'

'Better luck next time!'

'Measuring up to the judge's requirements'

'A faithful friend'

Keep Young and Beautiful

After 1945 care of "the aged" became a public topic. People were living longer, families were growing smaller and so the proportion of the older generation in the community was increasing.

Dagenham Council formed an Old People's Welfare Committee to promote a range of services including housing, clubs and holidays. Those who attended the clubs could play billiards and darts, attend handicraft classes or dance to their hearts' content.

In 1955, the Dagenham Meals on Wheels Service provided over 6,000 meals a year to the housebound. Domestic helps and district nurses also attended frail residents in their homes.

A visit to the circus by Beacontree Heath Old People's Club, 1955

'Our new home'
Woodlands Old People's Home, 1957

'Oh! I do like to be beside the seaside!',
An outing for Wantz Old Folk's Club, 1955

'Do I have to eat this?', A special 'Meals on Wheels' delivery

'On cue!'

A tea break at Fanshawe Old People's Club

'Down memory lane' – discussion group for old people at Oxlow Lane Clinic

A Winter's Tale

These photographs of winter tell us a tale of a different age. Before the huge impact of mass media on British culture, children were happy to amuse themselves in simple pastimes.

Due to the effects of rationing children did not expect elaborate or expensive Christmas gifts. Most families observed the traditional Christian festivities of Christmas. This involved attendance at church services, gathering around the table for dinner on Christmas Day and opening presents in front of a decorated tree. Celebrations in the schools included a visit from Father Christmas and a nativity play.

Bad weather severely affected the locality. Manual means of clearing the snow were much more labour intensive and less effective than today's modern snowplough.

'Bonfire Night', 1953

'O little town of Bethlehem',
St Chad's nativity play, 1957

'Christmas dinner'

'Frosty the Snowman.'

'Snow-bound'

'Snow-shovelling'
at Tolworth Parade, Chadwell Heath, 1955

'Christmas lights'

Mission Impossible!

Many of Egbert's photographic assignments are a complete puzzle to the modern viewer. Shrouded in the mystery of time, it is impossible to recapture the significance of these strange compositions. Council officials gave Mr Smart specific instructions to snap topical issues of his day but many images in this unique collection have lost their original meaning. Today we question why they were taken at all...

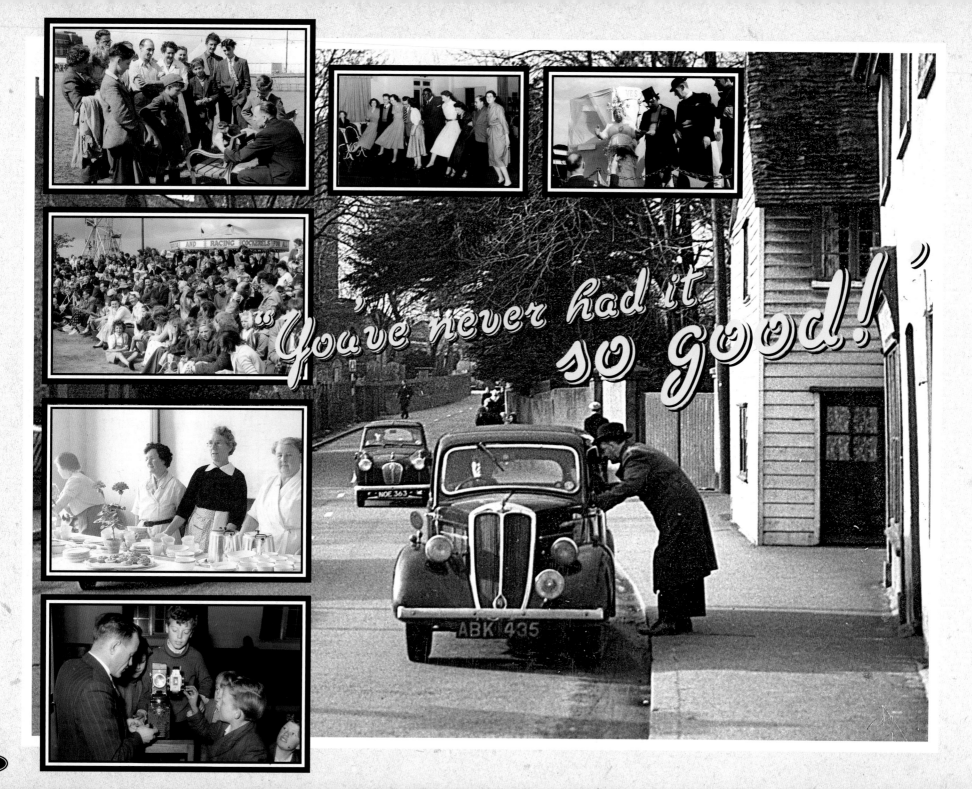

"You've never had it **so good!**"